Original title:

Footprints in the Sand

Copyright © 2025 Creative Arts Management OÜ
All rights reserved.

Author: Alec Davenport
ISBN HARDBACK: 978-1-80581-554-9
ISBN PAPERBACK: 978-1-80581-081-0
ISBN EBOOK: 978-1-80581-554-9

Imprints of a Journey

Tiny toes make marks, oh so neat,
As I trip over, can't find my feet.
Crabs look at me, they shake their claws,
Thinking, who made such clumsy flaws?

My flip-flops squeak with every step,
I dance like a penguin, no need to prep.
The seagulls laugh at my hapless fate,
While I just hope there's no shark on a plate!

The Lasting Mark of Time

In the grains, my foot finds a groove,
Each step is a joke, I can't help but move.
The tide comes in, with a splash and a swish,
Washing away my awkward foot wish.

A sandcastle toppled, my snack's in a heap,
Nibbled by seagulls, they want more to peep.
I stomp in revenge, but slip like a fool,
I guess that's what happens when you play by the pool!

Sands of Reflection

My shadow laughs as it skips by me,
Dancing in circles, as happy as can be.
I try to catch it, but it's quick on the draw,
Just like my friend, who slips on a straw!

With each step I take, I slip on a shell,
Falling in style, can't you just tell?
The sun sets low, but my antics still shine,
A comedic journey, oh how divine!

Ebb and Flow of Moments

I hop like a frog, with laughter so bright,
Each leap a misstep, what a silly sight!
Bubbles rise up, they tickle my toes,
As the waves swirl in with their playful shows.

A dog zooms past, it's chasing the breeze,
Tripping over treasures, with the greatest of ease.
We both look goofy, like we lost the race,
But in this madness, we've found our place!

Marks of the Wandering Heart

When you wander without a plan,
You might lose a flip-flop and a can.
The crabs will dance, the gulls will squawk,
As you leave behind your sandy chalk.

I once found a sandwich you'd think was a tease,
Hidden under a towel, covered in leaves.
And people stared at my crazy laugh,
As I scribbled my name in the sandy path.

Every wave tells a tale, or so they say,
Of a sock that was lost and a kid gone astray.
I'm pretty sure I saw a shoe take flight,
Chasing gulls under the pale moonlight.

So if you stumble on a sandy trail,
With munchies and giggles that never pale,
Just know it's a story, a mark of some sort,
From the wandering heart on its joyful fort.

A Chorus of Prints

In the sand, there's a song, a whimsical tune,
Of half-eaten snacks in the afternoon.
A boogie with toes, a twist and a twirl,
A comedy show in a sandy swirl.

The dog ran past, leaving chaos in tow,
As I tripped on my flip-flops, oh what a show!
The laughter erupted, the waves clapped along,
An ensemble of prints in this beachy throng.

With each little stumble, a giggle in sight,
As I waved at the kids who were flying their kites.
I danced with the tide like a wannabe pro,
Leaving marks of my moves in the sun's golden glow.

So gather your friends to the land where we play,
And leave your own stories in a bumbling way.
For in this great theater where laughter sings bright,
We're the chorus of prints in the warm sunlight.

Transient Trails

In the sun, we run, in flip-flops bright,
Leaving trails of laughter, what a sight!
Little bits of chaos scattered all around,
Oh, those tiny prints on sandy ground.

Seagulls squawk, and kids chase them away,
Running in circles, they're here to play.
Ice cream drips down, it makes quite a mess,
But who cares? We're here to impress!

With every step, we bring silly cheer,
Bouncing footprints, as they disappear.
As waves wash away our fun little traces,
We giggle and dance in these sunny spaces.

So here's to the paths that fade with the tide,
Each step a joyride, our hearts open wide.
With giggles and grins, we'll tread in the sun,
Chasing tomorrow, our laughter's not done.

Dance of the Ruins

In the cracked earth, I twirl and hop,
Who knew old stones could make me stop?
Dancing on ruins, I skip with flair,
Laughter echoing, floating in the air.

They say past whispers, but I hear a joke,
From crumbling walls, I hear them poke.
Each creaky step brings a comic reprieve,
With goofy jiggles, it's hard to believe!

Sunset paints stories in shades of gold,
While I trip on shadows, feeling bold.
A misfit in this ancient land so grand,
Yet, who cares when it's this much fun, understand?

So dance with me on this historical grind,
With each silly move, let's leave worries behind.
For in the ruins, we find pure delight,
Laughter is timeless, and so is the night.

The Language of the Land

Oh, the whispers of the earth beneath my toes,
Like ticklish secrets that nobody knows.
Braided trails in wildflower fields,
Unraveling stories that nature yields.

I clomp and stomp like I'm on a quest,
Searching for giggles, it's all for the best!
Every twig snaps, a chuckle in disguise,
With every new step, adventure arises.

From puddles of mud, to patches of grass,
The ground keeps talking, so let's not let it pass!
I speak in giggles, it's my secret sign,
As the earth giggles back, it's simply divine!

So in this wild world where we all dance free,
Let's tweet with the trees, and slide with glee.
The language of the land is pure, soft, and grand,
In every step, we're together—hand in hand.

Essence of a Stroll

A carefree saunter, skipping stones,
With each playful step, I make chuckling tones.
The path is a canvas, I paint my spree,
With footprints of laughter, wild and free.

Beneath the bright sun, my shirt's awry,
Crispy snacks crumble as I give a sigh.
Oh, salted chips and a fizzy cold drink,
In this backyard quest, we never outthink.

But what's that? A squishy blob on the ground!
Oh no! My shoe's stuck—what have I found?
With a leap and a giggle, I pull it free,
Life's full of surprises, just come stroll with me.

And every new corner reveals a wild grin,
Chasing the clouds and the laughter within.
So step by step, let's embrace the mess,
Each hilarious moment is pure happiness!

Nature's Diary

Each morning brings a tale to tell,
Of awkward critters and a shell.
A crab that dances by the shore,
Competing with the waves for more.

Seagulls squawk with snack attacks,
Stealing fries from unaware packs.
They strut and squawk, a silly show,
As beachgoers chase them, laughing so.

The sun sneaks up with a wink and grin,
While sunbathers are dozing, all tucked in.
Sunscreen flies like a confetti blast,
What a funny way to beat the heat fast!

Nature scribbles laughs in every way,
With sandy shorts from kids at play.
Laughter echoes like a joyful band,
This is how we write in nature's hand.

A Dance with the Ocean

The tides come in with a swish and slide,
As I attempt to surf with pride.
But gravity laughs, oh what a scene,
Down I go, splashed in salt and green.

The wave says, "Catch me if you can!"
While I wobble like a rubber band.
Fish giggle in their watery realm,
As I flounder like a captain overwhelmed.

My towel takes a getaway roll,
Up the beach, making its goal.
Chasing it down like a motion picture,
It twirls like it's got its own adventure.

With each return, guess what I find?
Sand in pockets, oh how unkind!
But laughter thrums in a playful song,
With the ocean, it feels like I belong.

Fleeting Glimpses

On the shore, I spot a shoe,
Whose owner thinks they've lost it too.
I wave and shout, 'Hey, look alive!'
That shoe's on a journey, the ocean's drive.

A toddler digs with laughter loud,
Creating castles, proud as a crowd.
Then comes the wave like a sneaky prank,
And down goes the kingdom, no time to thank!

The sun, it plays peek-a-boo,
Hiding behind the clouds, just for a view.
One second it's here, and gone in a dash,
Leaving sun-kissed moments, oh what a flash!

Life's a snapshot in grains of sand,
With giggles swirling like a joyful band.
These fleeting glimpses, funny and bright,
Capture the magic of beach day delight.

Echoing Footsteps

In the sandy stretch where we prance,
I hear a tune; let's start a dance!
With each step, the ground starts to sing,
Echoing moments like a joyful fling.

But wait, what's this? A squishing sound,
As I step on seaweed all around.
It makes a noise, quite weird and grand,
Like a sea monster is lending a hand.

My friend slips on a wet sandy patch,
A spectacle that's hard to match.
Kudos to the ocean for the great show,
And the sarcastic seagulls shouting, 'Whoa!'

With every step, a giggle shared,
All of our mishaps, tenderly paired.
As the waves dance back, and forth in time,
The laughter echoes in rhythm and rhyme.

Maritime Echoes

Two sailors adrift, with snacks in a bag,
They drift on a wave, doing an odd wag.
One leaps for a fish, but lands on his rear,
The ocean just laughs, as they munch on their beer.

A crab waves hello, with a pinch and a grin,
Our sailors just giggle, let the antics begin.
Each splash is a story, wild tales from the sea,
As their boat bobs along, oh, the fun is so free.

Chronicles of a Journey

Road trips are fun, with snacks in a pile,
But the map's upside down, oh, what a trial!
Mom's yelling at Dad, "You missed that last turn!"
The GPS giggles, 'till the tires all burn.

A cow in the field, just gives them a stare,
While kids in the back compete for fresh air.
They all sing along, but one's off the beat,
Does anyone care? No, they're riding a seat!

Rift of Memory

In the attic there's dust, and old shoes galore,
Left behind by the past, but oh, there's much more.
A box full of letters, and sweaters too tight,
They fit like a glove—if the glove's out of sight.

Grandma's old coat, with its buttons askew,
She wore it to dances, oh, what a view!
But now it's just hanging, collecting some slants,
As nephews give twirls, in their fun, goofy pants.

Lost in the Dunes

Oh, the desert is vast, with a sun that won't quit,
They thought they'd go hiking, now they just sit.
With sand in their shoes, and a laugh in each breath,
The good news is no one remembers their depth.

A tumbleweed rolls, laughing hard at their plight,
As they argue with shadows, who'll win the big fight?
Though lost in this mess, joy is never far,
In the dunes, life's a game; they're the star of the czar!

Shapes Left Behind

In the beach's golden spree,
There are prints of all that's free.
A crab's claw made a quirky mark,
Where it danced, oh what a lark!

A dodo came to take a stroll,
Leaving behind its jelly roll.
Seagulls laugh with flappy glee,
As they join in the sandy spree!

Across the Grain

I walked along the silken stretch,
Tripped over a buried wretch.
Something slimy glared at me,
Laughter's price—my dignity!

A toddler dashed with tiny toes,
Stirring up a sandstorm's blows.
Giggles painting the sunset hue,
As I slipped in a sandy stew!

The Passage of the Tide

The waves dance in and out like cats,
Leaving behind some funny spats.
A squid's sprawl, a fish's flail,
Nature's humor in every trail!

A dolphin jumped with silver flair,
As if it meant to comb its hair.
Then back to sea, it gave a wink,
While I pondered, "What's for drink?"

Starlit Paths

At night, the stars twinkle like jokes,
Telling tales to surf-side folks.
A raccoon wobbled on the sand,
While trying to grasp a conch in hand!

The moon chuckled at my fall,
As I tried to catch a bouncing ball.
With meteors showering bright and grand,
I'd swear my life's a comedy planned!

Echoes on the Shore

Sandcastles built, oh what a sight,
Only to crumble, a sad little plight.
Seagulls laughing, they steal my fries,
While I chase them with a frown, oh my, oh my!

Buries my toes in the warm golden grains,
Trying to dance, but I trip on my chains.
A wave rolls in, splashes my best hat,
Now it's a fish's new home - how 'bout that?

Imprints of Time

Walked on the beach, I lost my shoe,
Now I'm hopping like a kangaroo.
The tide comes in, erasing my hike,
Guess it's time for a swim, even if I don't like!

Struck by a crab, it pinched my toe,
Now I'm outnumbered, it's crab versus me, oh no!
With each step, the sand sticks like glue,
Maybe a towel would've been a good cue!

Traces Beneath the Waves

I tried to surf, but fell on my face,
Splashing around, I'm losing my grace.
A dolphin laughed, I swear he did grin,
As I bobbed like a cork, trying to swim!

Inflatable rings—my trusty sidekick,
Blown away by a breeze, it happened real quick.
A shell on my foot, snug as a clam,
Too bad, it's not dinner, just a bad jam!

Shadows of a Journey

Under the sun, I'm frying today,
Sunblock applied, but I forgot the spray.
I'm a lobster now, all red and sore,
Who knew sunbathing could feel like a chore?

Met a crab who wanted to dance,
But my fancy footwork ruined his chance.
With sandy sandwiches and soda cans,
My beachside picnic turned into quicksand plans!

The Dance of Water and Earth

Upon the shoreline, laughs abound,
As waves embrace, they swirl around.
With toes that tickle, and splashes high,
The sea tickles back, oh my, oh my!

The sand reports all the silly scenes,
Of clumsy pirouettes and missed routines.
A crab joins in with a sideways prance,
In this goofy, salty, sandy dance.

Frolicsome tides are the jokesters here,
Whispering secrets for all to hear.
Each wave a chuckle, each breeze a grin,
Who knew the coastline was this much fun?

So leap and hop, let your worries go,
Join the dance where wild ideas flow.
In the rhythm of surf, life spins unfurled,
Who knew Mother Nature could be so whirled?

Unseen Journeys

With every step on glittering shore,
A tale unfolds of adventures galore.
Barefoot strolls as the sun dips low,
Imagining journeys where feet dare to go.

The seabirds chuckle, as if to say,
'We've seen your antics every day!'
Sandcastles rise, then tumble down,
While crabbies giggle in their own little town.

Each grain a witness to laughter bright,
In the bootless wander of day and night.
So come along, let your spirit be free,
On these magical paths where can't-see's a spree.

So skip with glee, let worries be small,
You never know, you might just fall!
Into waves of fun and silly delight,
Where unseen journeys offer pure flight.

Waves of Remembrance

With each retreating tide there's a wink,
Reminding us not to overthink.
The beach throws back all the goof and jest,
A treasure chest of folly — oh, what a quest!

Shells whisper secrets, half-formed and odd,
Of narrow escapes and the luck of a plod.
A seagull giggles at yesterday's dance,
Stumbling on sandy romance and chance.

The sea sparkles with memories bright,
Of sunscreen mishaps and beach ball fights.
So gather your chuckles, let laughter ring,
As the waves of remembrance joyously swing.

For what's a beach trip without some misfire?
Where the sand becomes laughter, and we never tire.
Let's ride the crests of hilarious days,
As we soak in the splashes of whimsical waves.

Carved in Coastal Light

The sun grins wide on the wet, warm shore,
Crafting stories we cannot ignore.
As shadows dance with the rise and set,
A sandy scamper, I'll never forget.

Chasing down seagulls, what a big hoot,
They squawk and swirl, in a comical pursuit.
Yet they steal my snack while I trip and fall,
Oh, what a day! - laughter echoes the call.

The evening tide whispers silly tales,
Of mischief and grins, as daylight pales.
With each sandy outline, memories in flight,
Love is carved in this coastal light.

So remember this beach, with its quirk and flair,
Where laughter was woven in the salty air.
In each playful splash and every clumsy glide,
You'll find a world where joy can't hide.

The Story Each Grain Knows

Once I walked where the seagulls peck,
With shoes too tight, what the heck!
A dance on the beach, I tried to spin,
Tripped on my laces, fell in, what a win!

The grains all chuckled, as I got up,
I shooed them away, like an angry pup.
They whispered secrets of sandals and socks,
While I plotted my comeback – avoiding the rocks!

A crab was my judge, with a sharp little grin,
He clapped with delight as I spun in a spin.
I bowed to the crowd of the shells and the foam,
With laughter and waves, oh I felt quite at home!

Now every step leaves a tale in the dust,
Of comfy shoes or their absence, you trust.
The story goes on, with each joyful stride,
As grains of the beach keep the funny inside!

Waves and Writings

I wrote my name with a stick in the sand,
Hoped the ocean would take it, with a gentle hand.
But the waves had their plans, oh what a ruckus,
Swallowed my name, left no trace, just a circus!

The tide went high, and I started to fret,
Are oceans in on it? I bet they can act yet.
They giggled, they chuckled, with gulls sharing quips,
As I chased my own words with wet, sandy grips!

I tried again, using seashells for flair,
Only to find they were taking my hair.
With a splash and a laugh, I gave in to fate,
My thoughts now afloat, perhaps I should wait!

The waves keep on rolling, my stories are lost,
In a game of tag, but it's all worth the cost.
Each splash in the sea hides a grin or a wink,
As I dance with the tide, there's no time left to think!

Tracks in the Twilight

As the sun set low, I took a big stride,
Leaving behind me a line, what a ride!
I marched like a penguin, with arms open wide,
Thought I'd impress the stars; they just sighed!

The twilight giggled, with colors in hand,
Painting my journey across the soft sand.
Each mark that I made, a silly charade,
As shadows grew longer, my feet misplayed!

Oh, the clumsy ballet of the evening was sweet,
With a side step here and a twirl on my feet.
The sand tickled toes, as I stumbled around,
My dance for the moon left a laugh, not a sound!

But as night wrapped around, and I took my last bow,
I wondered which star would see me right now.
Would they giggle at my tracks, all jumbled and weird?
Or send me some help, since I clearly veered?

Eternal Remnants

In the morning light, I strolled down the shore,
Each step left a mark, but oh, there's more!
The tide had a laugh as it danced on by,
Erasing my traces, oh why oh why?

A banana peel caught my heel with a snap,
I stumbled and tumbled, oh what an unwrap!
With laughter from crabs, oh the joyful din,
My mishap became part of their ridiculous grin!

Then I found a starfish, with wisdom to share,
He said, "Never look back, life's not meant for despair!"
But one sandcastle later, it crumbled and fell,
"Absurdity reigns, far better than well!"

So each day I wander, creating my art,
With giggles and tumbles, that's where I start.
Though the waves will erase what I leave on the land,
The laughter of sand is my eternal brand!

The Path that Once Was

A trail of mishaps woven wide,
Where clumsy toes did often slide.
The tide waves chuckled, oh so clear,
At the antics of the beachside deer.

With every step, a toe would hide,
Beneath the waves, they could confide.
The shells would giggle, sand would laugh,
As I danced away on my behalf.

The ocean whispered secrets near,
Of epic fails, oh what a sphere!
My path, a story, wrote itself,
Just like that old forgotten shelf.

But when the tide would come to claim,
My silly strides, a fleeting fame.
Yet still I laugh, and oh I prance,
As the sea plots another dance.

Sea Salt Memories

With a pinch of salt and a splash of fun,
I skipped along, thought I'd just run.
But waves crept in, on a sneaky quest,
And soaked my shoes, oh life's a jest!

I chased the seagulls, thought I was slick,
But tripped on a crab, it was quite the trick.
They screeched and squawked, my ego fell,
As shells applauded my humor spell.

The sun set low, painting the sky,
As I looked for answers to passersby.
'Why are we here?' I yelled unclear,
The ocean just chuckled, never fear!

So here's to those who lose their way,
In the midst of laughter, come what may.
For every slip on salty land,
A memory made, a joke well planned.

Erosion of Existence

In the battle with time, sand wins the game,
As my sunburn fades, it's all quite the same.
I lay on the beach, turning bronze like toast,
While sand plays tag, a troublesome host.

The waves come in, and I think they conspire,
To steal my sunglasses and add to my mire.
They whisper sweet tales of ages gone by,
While I search my bag for a snack on the sly.

Oh look! That castle, once grand and proud,
Now a pile of rubble, lost in the crowd.
The tide rolls in with a giggling roar,
And takes my dreams for an ocean tour.

But I smile wide, I'll build anew,
With each grain of sand, creativity grew.
For nothing can stop this jester profound,
Not the sea nor the sun can keep me down.

Gentle Etchings in Grain

As I scrawl with toes in the golden dust,
The grains of history, I find a trust.
Each letter, misspelled, tells a tale quite absurd,
Like a limerick lost, or a poet disturbed.

The gulls look down, with a puzzled expression,
At my goofy scribbles, a fine misdirection.
They chirp with laughter, my calligraphy,
Is proof I'm not bound for a gallery.

The sunset dims, and I dream of a book,
With chapters of laughter, come take a look!
Each page a memory, a smile, a grin,
Of sandcastles built where the waves begin.

So come join the fun, there's mischief to make,
Life's too short for perfection's mistake.
With gentle etchings, let joy expand,
In this quirky story written in sand.

Stories Written by the Sea

Waves whisper tales in the breeze,
A crab tries to dance, but he trips with ease.
Seagulls gossip, all in a flap,
While a starfish lounges, taking a nap.

Shells gather secrets, they giggle and prattle,
As kids build castles, they're on a new battle.
A wave swooshes in, much to their dismay,
It laughs at their towers, then sweeps them away.

Tired of surfing, a dolphin starts to tease,
As a fish flips around, seeking out a free cheese.
The sun sets slowly, in colors so bright,
Even the seaweed is ready for night.

The tide comes and goes, with a mischievous grin,
Leaving behind laughter, a watery din.
Let's join the fun as the tide pulls away,
Only to return, for a splashy replay!

Castaway Dreams

A bottle rolled in with a message unknown,
A pirate's treasure, or just a lost cone?
With coconuts dancing, they form a parade,
As crabs don their hats, eager to invade.

The palm trees are swaying, as if they could sing,
While a seagull swoops down, hoping for bling.
A castaway grumbles, with a sandwich to munch,
While some eager fish eagerly join for lunch.

Island life's quirky, with laughter and cheer,
A coconut crash, oh what a great year!
The sun beams down, bringing smiles with each ray,
Even the waves giggle, they just want to play.

A treasure map drawn on a napkin so bold,
Leads to a trove of glitter and gold.
But what they find, oh what a surprise!
Just seashells and laughter, a feast for the eyes.

Memory's Footfalls

Tiny strides shuffle across the warm shore,
Leaving behind echoes of giggles and lore.
A dog zooms past, chasing the tide,
While kids play tag, shrieking with pride.

Grandpa's old tales swirl in the air,
Of mermaids and pirates, armor they wear.
The sun's golden rays sprinkle joy all around,
As kites fly high over soft, sandy ground.

A puzzled crab plays hide and seek,
Beneath a damp rock, it peeks and they squeak.
The seaweed waves and joins the dance,
Adding to whimsy—a froggy romance.

Driftwood sculptures stand tall and strange,
Each telling stories, a whimsical range.
With laughter and echoes, the moments align,
Creating a tapestry, vivid and fine.

The Draw of the Dunes

Sand dunes stretch far, with heights so grand,
Like mountains of sugar, kissed by sea hand.
A tumbleweed rolls, as wind gives a shout,
While kids race to slide, no worries, no doubt.

Seagull takes flight, with a snack in its claw,
A sandwich, upside down? Oh, that's quite the flaw!
The dunes hold their secrets, tales buried deep,
Of laughter and tumbles, and memories to keep.

Picnics are spread under sunny skies bright,
With ants crashing parties, what a silly sight!
Unexpected finds, like lost flip-flops and shoes,
All captured in giggles with the fluttering blues.

At day's end, shadows dance on the crest,
While everyone finds that home is the best.
In moonlight, the dunes will whisper and hum,
A melody waiting, for wishes to come.

Whirls of Reflection

In the surf, I saw a trace,
An imprint of a silly face.
I laughed out loud at the sight,
A fish splashed me, oh what a fright!

Stomping along with big wide strides,
Pretending that my troubles hide.
But the tide came in with a grin,
And washed away my little win.

Like a rogue wave at a fiesta,
I danced and tripped, oh what a jester!
The gulls just giggled overhead,
As I lunged like I was misled.

So here I am, a comical sprite,
Wandering in laughable light.
Chasing after waves with glee,
Forget my shoes, just let me be!

A Pilgrimage of Solitude

On this lonely beach I trod,
In search of peace, or maybe a pod.
I spotted a crab with a scowl,
And whispered, mate, you're in a howl!

With each step, a new friend mocks,
A seagull stole my sandwich, no shocks!
A meditative stroll turned into chase,
A feast for one became a food race.

Sandcastles rise, dreams unfold,
Then the tide comes, brazen and bold.
My castle a moistened heap of goo,
I chuckled, oh who knew?

I'll wander forever, just me and the sea,
In solitude, it's just pure comedy.
With laughter echoing wide and bright,
My pilgrimage is sheer delight!

The Fade of Time's Touch

Moments slip away like water,
My sunburn's bright, oh how it's hotter!
With every step, a memory glows,
And the sand shifts where nobody goes.

Tick-tock goes the watch on my wrist,
But I'm too busy sipping a fizz.
The clock is a pirate, stealing my day,
Yet I'm here in this bubbly ballet.

I wondered, can a hermit crab dance?
His shell said yes, he took a chance!
With each twist, I laughed and spun,
Moments fade, but smiles weigh a ton.

So here I am, lost in a chuckle,
While the ocean swirls in a playful shuffle.
Old time may fade, but I'll stay bold,
In this laughter, treasure untold!

Written in the Tides

When the tide ebbs away from the shore,
I find old jokes and laughter galore.
A seashell whispers secrets of glee,
As I dance with sand, wild and free.

Shells hold stories of laughs and yells,
From tourists like me, with sand-filled hotels.
The ocean snickers as it spills,
Waves crack jokes, giving me thrills.

Every splash brings a ticklish tick,
A slippery dance, oh what a trick!
I shake and wiggle, what a delight,
As the water giggles into the night.

With spray and foam, my day's a blast,
No footprints left, fun's amassed.
In the tides' embrace, I'm never a bore,
With laughter echoing forevermore!

Spills of the Sea

As I strolled by the sea, oh what a sight,
My drink took a tumble, my face full of fright.
The waves laughed in rows, as they danced by my feet,
I paused for a moment, not ready to greet.

With flip-flops a-flinging, I slipped in the surf,
My goodness, what balance! I gave it a smirk.
The kelp played my friend, wrapping 'round my big toe,
While seagulls conspired, they watched me for show.

Now my beach day's a tale, full of slips and of spills,
With laughter and splashes, I'm chasing the chills.
The tides crash in glee, calling me back for more,
Each wave brings new jokes, that I can't ignore.

Marks of Mindfulness

On a stroll through the sand, I found quite a mess,
My toes dug in deep, what a wonderful stress.
A crab with a wink scuttled right by my heel,
In this mindful moment, I learned how to feel.

With each tiny step, I thought of my plight,
Those marks were not mine, but I made them just right.
Shapes dancing around like my thoughts on the go,
A hippo? A kite? Or a squiggly foe?

As I laughed at my art, a seagull surprised,
Took my snack with a hop, I was dumbfounded, wide-eyed.
Yet each grain that I left was a whisper of cheer,
In this sandy art show, I've got nothing to fear.

Between Here and There

Where the sun meets the foam, I'm caught in a sway,
Between here and there, my worries float away.
I balance on edges where nonsense is king,
In the silent ballet, oh what joy it can bring.

Each step's a small venture, like tiptoeing on air,
With laughter as my guide, I don't have a care.
The tide called my name, with a splash and a tease,
And the sea's silly winks made my laughter freeze.

So I dance with the waves, in this playful embrace,
Lost in my thoughts, yet I can't help but chase.
Between giggles and splashes, I skip with the tide,
With a smile on my face, I abandon my pride.

The Sand's Caress

Oh, the grit and the grain, a warm hug to my toes,
The shore's soft embrace, where the silly tide flows.
With shells as my friends and the breeze like a song,
I revel in laughter, where the silly belongs.

I planted my feet, let the waves pull me near,
But slipped on a starfish, oh what a grand cheer!
The sand yelled, 'Get up!' with a tickle and tease,
While the gulls took my chips, oh, what a grand wheeze!

In the midst of this chaos, I learned how to play,
With each unexpected trip, I'd chase worries away.
The warmth of the sun and the surf's merry dance,
I smile at the ocean, in its silly expanse.

Whispers of the Wanderer

Strolling by the shore so wide,
Each step a tale, no place to hide.
The tide loses track of my rubber shoe,
Laughing at the mischief that I dare to do.

A seagull giggles, it's quite a scene,
While I fumble with sand like a silly machine.
Oh, the shells and crabs seem to conspire,
To turn my walk into a comedy choir.

Sandy snacks cling to my knee,
My best friend laughs, 'You look like a tree!'
With limbs all adorned in beachy charms,
Who knew I'd cause such laughs with my clumsy arms?

Shoes left behind, now soaking wet,
Chasing waves, a hilarious bet.
Who knew wanderers could make such a fuss?
The sea just chuckles, "Come walk with us!"

Of Sand and Spirit

With each bouncy step, I attempt to glide,
But the grains beneath just laugh and slide.
Jumping with joy, my shoes take a flight,
As the sea waves hello, in the sun's warm light.

Sand angels form where I flop and sway,
Looking rather silly all through the day.
Crabs point and snicker from their sandy homes,
While I wiggle and jiggle in my sandy foams.

"Catch me if you can," I yell to the breeze,
But my flip-flops betray me, oh, where's the ease?
Who knew a stroll could turn into a race,
With the ocean helping me lose my grace?

The sand's a comedian, it rolls me around,
Chasing seagulls is really quite profound.
Hidden treasures? Just sandy shoes!
A laughter-filled journey, so much to lose!

Subtle Marks of Moments

In the golden light, I prance and leap,
Leaving markers, oh, so deep.
A twist, a turn, why can't I dance?
The sea throws a curveball; it's all by chance.

Sandy toes hidden under waves,
The ocean tugs; oh, how it braves!
'Just walk normally!' my friend would insist,
But the sand, like a jester, can't be dismissed.

A stumble here, a splash over there,
Turning this beach into my comedy lair.
Crabs in rows call me out on my game,
While the sea laughs beside them, calling my name.

Moments captured, each slip a delight,
In laughter and joy, I ignite the night.
With a skip and a hop, oh what a spree,
These moments of silly shall always be free!

Remnants in the Breeze

Strutting my stuff, I try to impress,
But the wind takes hold of my beachy dress.
With laughter escaping and hair all askew,
I'm the jest of the sea, it's all too true.

The shells roll their eyes, say, "Not again!"
"Sand in the hair, oh where's our zen?"
A flip here, a flop there, a laugh on a wave,
This beach is my stage, and I'm feeling brave.

My friend's lost her hat to the ocean's tease,
And the sunlight beams down with a cheeky breeze.
With each quirky moment, my heart takes flight,
The fun of these antics makes everything right.

So here we go, let's embrace the mad,
With memories of laughter, the best we've had.
In every giggle, every swish and sway,
The remnants of joy will never fray.

A Trail of Feelings

In the beach breeze, I danced so fine,
Until I tripped on one of my lines.
My flip-flops flew, oh what a sight,
Made the seagulls cackle with pure delight.

Waves chuckled too, and splashed my toes,
As I wobbled back, striking comic poses.
Each laugh, a step on this sandy spree,
Oh, the joys of my clumsy spree!

A crab joined in, with a sideways strut,
As I tried to keep my balance, not to glut.
We shared a dance, with all our grace,
A silly waltz in this sandy place.

So I left my mark, funny and bright,
A comedy sketch in the morning light.
In every grain, a grin I've spread,
While laughing loudly, I'm glad I tread!

Heartbeats on the Horizon

On this shoreline where silliness reigns,
I tried to jog; it brought such pains.
Tripped over shells, did a wild spin,
The seagulls laughed, 'Let the jokes begin!'

With each awkward step, my heart's little race,
I looked quite the fool in this goofy place.
But every tumble was met with cheers,
As waves rolled in, silencing fears.

A dog came bounding, chasing his ball,
I dodged that pup, but it turned to a fall.
Rolling in sand, I giggled so loud,
Made quite the spectacle, oh yes, I'm proud!

As the sun set low, with laughter so bright,
Each heartbeat danced like bubbles in flight.
A memory formed in evening's embrace,
With giggles and joy, oh, what a race!

Sunlit Pathways

Down the sunny beach, I skipped with flair,
Playing hopscotch with my own reckless air.
Each step a challenge, each toe a thrill,
As I hopped past jellyfish that gave me a chill.

The sun beamed down, gleaming on my skin,
While my fancy dance turned into a spin.
Two kids on surfboards laughed at my show,
They flipped and flopped; I can't quite flow.

With every twist, and dive into sand,
I lost my balance, oh isn't it grand?
I rolled like a log, from shore to the sea,
A real comedian, just look at me!

These sunlit pathways spark joy and delight,
As I stumble and giggle, through day and night.
In this silly dance, I write my own song,
On the sunny shores, where every step's wrong.

The Art of Erosion

On the beach I learned, in a whimsical way,
That slipping and sliding can make your day.
I tried to sculpt castles, oh what a mess,
A mound of sand, my own sandy stress.

As the tide crept in, my dream washed away,
Funny how Mother Nature came to play.
I waved at the waves, as they took my dream,
With a splash and a laugh — it was quite the theme!

Seagulls swooped down, to check on my plight,
I flailed at them wildly, what a silly sight!
With my bucket and shovel, I chased them around,
While my sand throne melted right into the ground.

So I left with a smile, a heart full of cheer,
Embracing my failures, with nothing to fear.
Life's art of erosion is fun if you try,
To laugh at your sandcastles as they wave goodbye!

A Traveler's Ghost

In the sun, I dance and prance,
With steps that lead to mischance.
A phantom here, just to amuse,
I trip on waves, I can't refuse.

Each stride I take is full of glee,
While jellyfish high-five with me.
I'm lost, but what a lovely ride,
With giggles echoing at my side.

The sand's my stage, I sashay free,
As crabs and seagulls laugh at me.
I vanish quick when tides come near,
But not before I shed a tear.

Oh, what a joy, this ghostly play,
Where laughter shines, and troubles sway.
I'll haunt this shore with every jest,
A merry soul, I love my quest.

The Story Beneath My Feet

With each soft step, a tale unfolds,
Of sandy highways in sunlight golds.
Crabs wave hello, in coats of bling,
While I recount the joy in spring.

Here's a tale of the shoe that slipped,
Into a wave, and got quite dipped.
It swam away with a splashy grin,
Leaving only my sock to spin.

The stories written, oh-so-fine,
By waves and winds that intertwine.
I chuckle at every silly feat,
Oh, the whispers soft beneath my feet.

As tides come in, they tease and play,
Erasing tales of my clumsy way.
Yet with each wave, a new story's born,
In the sand, my laughter is adorned.

Logan's Last Walk

Logan marched with zeal, so spry,
Till he met a rogue seagull fly.
With a cheeky peck, he lost a shoe,
Now it's seagull toast, who even knew?

Each step brought giggles, oh-so-sweet,
As shells and seaweed danced at his feet.
With every stride, the sea would tease,
Saying, "Come play! Swim with ease!"

But oh! He slipped on a starfish bright,
Tumbling down in a comical sight.
The waves laughed loud, a raucous cheer,
As Logan grinned through salty fear.

His last walk was a merry spree,
With laughter splitting the salty spree.
He left behind tales that would echo wide,
Of sea lanes crossed and his wild ride.

Lapping Lullabies of the Sea

The waves would sing as they kissed the shore,
With a lullaby that begged for more.
I jigged and jived, my feet so light,
In a grand ballet under the moonlight.

Crab choirs sang in shells so bright,
While fishy dancers twirled in flight.
I tried to join, but they swam away,
Leaving me in a funny display.

Their giggles mingled with the foam,
As I lost my balance and called it home.
The sand got caught, in my hair and shoes,
A sandy nest, oh, what a ruse!

But with each wave's gentle sway,
I found my peace in the ocean's play.
So here I laugh, to the sea's refrain,
In this wacky world, I go insane.

Reflections on Wind-swept Beige

In the golden grains I tread,
I slipped on jelly instead.
A seagull laughed as I flailed,
My grace and poise have surely failed.

With every step, I trip and slide,
Beige wonderland, my joy and pride.
The ocean chuckles, waves in glee,
'Careful there, don't drown like me!'

Steps Left in Solitude

A lonely stroll along the shore,
I danced a jig, I lost my chore.
The crabs joined in, they mocked my move,
As laughter rang, my worries soothed.

A flip-flop flew, like a bird in flight,
Chasing a shell, oh what a sight!
Who knew the tides would echo back,
'You brought that shoe? You better pack!'

Faded Echoes of Adventure

In sandy lands, where tales are spun,
I found a treasure chest, oh what fun!
Filled with socks that I lost last week,
And a rubber duck, all yellow and sleek.

A pirate parrot squawked with cheer,
'You found my loot, I'll wait right here!'
I grabbed a shell and said, 'Not today,'
And danced on my way, with a smile to sway.

The Journey's Ghost

A wisp of wind, it howls with grace,
'That's my sandwich!' it seems to chase.
Invisible friends in need of a snack,
A picnic thief, now that's the knack.

Every laugh, a mile I've left,
Through grains of joy, oh what a heft!
'Who eats here?' I turned to see,
A ghost of laughter, just like me!

Mementos of a Closure

On a beach I trudged with grace,
Leaving marks in a funny place.
Seagulls laughed, I knew their game,
Each step a story, none the same.

My cousin tried to run and leap,
Got stuck in mud, went down in heaps!
We said goodbye to shoes and pride,
Our giddy giggles were bona fide.

A crab strolled by, gave me a wink,
I questioned if he'd had too much drink.
We shared a moment, what a sight,
Me, the human, him, the delight!

In the end, a sandy tale we weave,
As memories stick, we laugh and leave.
Those traces fade with the tide's embrace,
But oh, those chuckles we still replay!

Waves of Brief Encounters

At the ocean's edge, oh what a catch!
Met a dolphin who loved to scratch.
He flipped, he flopped, with quite the flair,
I shouted back, "Hey, don't you dare!"

A surfer slipped, went down like toast,
He shouted, "Help! I'm being grossed!"
We roared with laughter, a wild affair,
Sand filled our shoes, but we didn't care.

The tide would wash away our fun,
Yet every wave brought more to run.
Life's a comedy, just pick your role,
With every splash, we'd lose control.

In each moment, quirks hold sway,
While nature laughs, we dance and play.
And though the shore's a fleeting friend,
Our silly tales will never end!

Serene Passages in Time

The beach was still, I wobbled in,
With sunblock slathered on my chin.
An old man chuckled, said, "What's that?"
I blinked and fell—impressive splat!

A toddler ran, arms open wide,
Locked eyes with waves, oh what a ride!
We tumbled down, and clumsy we fell,
A dance of mischief, a sandy spell.

The sunsets glow, a perfect tease,
With our laughter carried on the breeze.
Moments freeze in the salty air,
As time tickles us, unaware.

Each grain of sand, a giggle saved,
In quiet joy, our spirits braved.
With silly tales, we lay and dream,
On shores adorned by laughter's gleam!

Sandcastles of the Forgotten

We built a castle big and grand,
With towers made of golden sand.
A wave approached with mischief's smirk,
Took our work without a perk!

A child nearby started to cheer,
"Look, it's a moat, oh dear, oh dear!"
We giggled as our dreams took flight,
While shells became our knight's delight.

An elder strolled with dog in tow,
Tipped his hat, said, "Time to go!"
But not before he stepped right in,
Our castle fell—now that's a win!

As day turned night, we watched the tide,
The laughter rippled, deep inside.
In sandy graves, our joys remain,
With burst of laughter, life's great gain!

A Journey's End

Once I tripped on a grain of sand,
My flip-flop flew; oh, it took a stand!
Waves laughed aloud, splashing with glee,
"You should've packed umbrellas, not a tree!"

At the shore, I slipped and fell,
A crab skittered off, wishing me well.
Seagulls squawked, as if to say,
"That's the best show we've had today!"

With shells in hand, my pockets are full,
Each one a memory, some quite dull.
But among them all, a pebble shines,
"Why didn't I leave it to the brines?"

As the sun sets, I wave goodbye,
To the silly antics, I can't deny.
My journey's end, with laughter so grand,
Forever engraved in this heavenly sand.

Silent Conversations with the Sea

The water whispers, 'You're looking quite silly,'
Chasing waves like a kid, oh what a frilly!
I splashed and I spluttered, a sight to behold,
The ocean laughed loudly, its humor quite bold.

In my bucket, small treasures I found,
Plastic toys mixed with shells all around.
The sea teased and tugged at my makeshift chair,
"Next time, my friend, try not to despair!"

Someone's flip-flop, I claimed as my prize,
It flopped off my foot; oh, what a surprise!
Driftwood like sculptures, all twisted and bent,
The sea's got a sense of humor, heaven-sent.

As I gaze at the waves, they wink back with cheer,
Ready to share more laughs every year.
Silent conversations, all giggles and high,
With the sea's magic touch, oh, how time does fly!

Nature's Gentle Memory

Each grain a story, a tickle, a jest,
Sandals in hand, what a funny quest!
The sand teased my toes, cold and so nice,
One slip and a swerve—oh, how to think twice!

The tide rolls in, it's quite the surprise,
Pulling my towel, to my great demise!
I shout to the sea, 'You can't have my snack!'
Yet here comes a wave, with a sneaky attack.

Seagulls above, plotting some heists,
Diving for chips, they act like brats, oh so light!
Each giggle and wiggle, a jaunt in the breeze,
With nature's gentle hands, laughter's all I seize.

As night comes with stars, the memories hum,
Each laugh in the air, where the wild things come.
Nature's gentle memory, wrapped in a bow,
With waves of pure joy, there's always a show!

Songs of the Surf

The surf sings sweetly, a melody grand,
Complaining about shells littering the land.
I bop to the rhythm, even dance a bit,
The sand's my dance floor, oh what a hit!

Seagulls take turns, belting out tunes,
While I trip over treasures, under the moons.
A crab join the chorus, what a surprise,
Snapping its claws, as if to critique my size!

The waves crash and laugh, it's quite the affair,
Bubbling with humor, no troubles to bear.
I shout out my verses, the sea sings along,
Creating a ballad, the waves can't go wrong.

As the sun dips low, I hum with delight,
"What a funny day!" I whisper to night.
With songs from the surf, still ringing in air,
I'll treasure this laughter, forever to share.

Sketches on the Tidal Canvas

The tide rolled in with a cheeky grin,
Melting my shapes and causing a spin.
A baby crab danced, then ran in retreat,
While I stumbled and waved, with sand on my feet.

Seagulls above with their mocking call,
Watching my antics, they laughed hard and tall.
One snatched my sandwich, oh what a thief!
I chased with sand in my shorts, pure disbelief.

Each little wave holds a giggling surprise,
As seaweed wraps round like nature's disguise.
I tried to impress, but fell on my rear,
The ocean just chuckled, 'I'll take that, my dear!'

So here I create laughs with each splash and slip,
A canvas of giggles on this sunny trip.
With sketches of folly, I leave my mark,
A gallery of chuckles, where me and the sea spark.

Wanderer's Heart on the Coast

A wanderer's heart beats loud by the shore,
But in the sand, I've left so much more.
A dance of missteps, oh what a sight,
I flirted with waves in a playful fight.

My sandals flew off, I tripped on a shell,
Every tumble just added to this quirky spell.
I waved to a dolphin, it laughed at my fall,
While crabs in tuxedos formed a waltzing ball.

The breeze just roared like it saw my strife,
In this slapstick show called my coastal life.
Each wave an encore, what a silly joke,
I'll bow with a flourish—give me that poke!

With laughter as currency, I paid my way,
Trading my clumsiness for a beach day sway.
Come join the spectacle, where bliss reigns supreme,
In the wandering heart that dances in dreams.

Traces Beneath the Waves

Beneath the waves, my antics float by,
A treasure of blunders beneath this blue sky.
An octopus chuckled, seven arms in the air,
While I wobbled and splashed without a care.

The shells whispered secrets of clumsy past falls,
As I searched for my lost shoe, oh what a brawl!
Anemones giggled, their tickles a tease,
While I flailed about like a ship caught in breeze.

Each wave that crashed seemed to point and snicker,
I put on a show, just trying to flicker.
But the tide had its plans for my frolicsome spree,
As it pulled at my shorts, 'Come play, just be free!'

So even in chaos, I left my sweet trace,
With laughter and joy painted all over this place.
In a world full of giggles, I found my own way,
With prints of pure fun that will never decay.

Ephemeral Impressions

On the shore, as I pranced, I made quite the scene,
My dance was a blend of awkward and keen.
The sand clung to my legs like a friendly embrace,
While I waved at the waves, lost in my chase.

With a flick of my toes, I noticed a fish,
It darted away like it granted my wish.
The gulls overhead formed a snicker brigade,
As I twirled, then tripped, like a human charade.

In this temporary world of imprints and glee,
Each error was laughter, just the ocean and me.
Falling face-first, with a splash and a grin,
I wondered if the tide would invite me back in.

So here's to the moments that slip through our hands,
Like bubbles that burst on this whimsical sands.
With every odd jig and each funny display,
I leave my impressions—forever at play!

The Mark of Passage

On the beach where seashells gleam,
A crab scuttles, chasing a dream.
I made my mark with a squishy shoe,
But the tide erases it, oh what to do!

Seagulls squawk and bomb dive low,
While I strut like a crab—here we go!
Each step I take is a wobbly dance,
Fish laugh, I hope, they give me a chance!

A toddler giggles, chasing his hat,
While I trip and play like a silly cat.
The ocean chuckles at my clumsy stunts,
I wave to the waves as they splatter my fronts!

In the end, I'm just part of the show,
Making memories, that much I know.
Even if they wash away like sand,
They'll still bring a smile, oh isn't it grand?

Fleeting Echoes

Waves whisper secrets, loud yet absurd,
As my flip-flops squawk like a flock of birds.
With each step, a splash, I sing out loud,
My sun-kissed adventure, I feel so proud!

But oh dear tide, why so quick to erase?
The giggling crabs, they're winning this race!
I draw little hearts, but the sea fills them in,
A canvas of laughter, fresh from the bin!

Seashells compete with the stories I share,
Each one a treasure, laid out with care.
But instead, I trip, with grace undefined,
Oh, laughter of dolphins, how sweet and kind!

Lasting impressions, yet, here I stand,
As the waves play tag with my fleeting hand.
They turn my odd dance into frothy spray,
Leaving a memory, come what may!

Under the Sky's Embrace

Under the sky, all fuzzy and wide,
I prance like a penguin, without a guide.
The sun takes pictures, whilst ducks offer tips,
As I tango with sea foam and dream of fish lips!

With sandals that squeak like they've lost their fight,
I strut my stuff, oh, what a sight!
An octopus winks, I wink back in fun,
While jellyfish giggle beneath the sun!

Seagulls attempt to steal my last fry,
But I'm an ace, I just wave goodbye!
The tide gives a nudge, pulls me to dance,
My splashing and laughing, oh what a chance!

So here I leap, with laughter and flair,
Dancing with shadows, without a care.
Under a sky where the joy never ends,
I find my rhythm, with sea as my friend.

Breaths of the Ocean

The ocean exhales with a salty embrace,
As I prance about, what a silly case!
My beach ball slips, a runaway glee,
Chased by a wave, oh come back to me!

Sandy toes wiggle, a dance of delight,
As seaweed's my tie—as wrong as it's right.
I craft a fine castle; it's tall like a tower,
But the next wave's a beast, what an empowering hour!

With laughter like bubbles that tickle and pop,
I embrace the chaos; I'll never stop!
A pelican steals my sandwich pretzel,
I just laugh and shout, "Hey, it's a feast for the vessel!"

As sunset arrives with a flicker and hue,
I leave my mark—but not just a few!
For in every wave, every breeze that I meet,
Are the giggles of joy that make life so sweet.

Beyond the Shoreline

Upon the waves, I built a case,
For seashells and sand, a clammy place.
But each big wave soon smashed my prize,
And now I'm left with seagull sighs.

The jellyfish dance, oh what a show,
I stepped on one, thought it was dough.
With a squelch and a squirm, it made its wish,
To swim away fast, my beach day swish!

As crabs retreat with pinching claws,
I chase them down, just because.
With buckets of flops, I catch my glee,
But they march away—oh, they're too free!

Yet on the sand, I dig and twirl,
Bury my foot and do a whirl.
Oh beach, you're silly, you stole my fun,
With laughter echoing as I run!

Fading Resonance

A flip-flop here, a sandal there,
The shore's a minefield; tread with care!
Oh, the splashes and giggles all around,
As I trip and faceplant on the ground.

Seagulls dive with chatter-filled sass,
They steal my chips; they're such a brash class.
While I'm busy scolding the crafty team,
A crab steals my sandwich, or so it would seem!

Kites fly high, but I'm on the ground,
My hat blows off; where's that clumsy sound?
Chasing my headwear, I stumble and fall,
I'm the beach clown—tripping through it all!

With laughter and waves, the sun dips low,
Running away from my worries, aglow.
The sand may not keep my secrets or tricks,
But it surely records all my comical slips!

The Heart of the Beach

Where then did my ice cream cone go?
Oh, the sun melted it all in a row!
With sticky hands and a curious dash,
I ran to the waves, ankle-deep splash!

The children giggle, watch me lose my grip,
As I slip on the edge and take a dip.
I wave for help, but it's all in vain,
They just laugh at my soggy disdain!

Then dolphins cheer, flipping through the air,
I tried to join in, but my flaps have no flair.
Flailing around like a beached-up whale,
I get a round of applause for this epic fail!

Yet who cares about grace when laughter's the aim?
I'll keep bringing joy, even without fame.
For in the shenanigans, life finds its role,
At the heart of the beach, I'm the star of the soul!

Impressions Lost to Time

As I scan the sand, what do I see?
A chorus of marks that are just not me!
From kids with their toys, to dogs in full sprint,
I ponder my legacy—oh, what a hint!

I tried to make castles, taller than tall,
But the tide came in; oh, it was a brawl.
Waves washed my dreams with a foamy embrace,
Voices of laughter, "Let's all join the race!"

There's a deep dive here, a dance from the barn,
Seashells are clinking like odd pots and pans.
But my best-kept secrets—what remains?
A shoddy pair of flip-flops, like battle stains!

Yet memories linger like a saltwater kiss,
In this land of giggles, how could I miss?
With every mishap that roams with a breeze,
I'll cherish these moments, oh, yes, please!

Silent Stories by the Sea

Whispers of laughter float on by,
As I slip in the mud, oh my!
Seagulls giggle as I slide,
What a sight, I can't abide!

Waves tease my toes, splashing near,
Telling tales of ruckus here.
I trip on a shell, oh so sly,
A fish winks, and I just sigh.

Sandcastles rise, fall with a clunk,
A crab steals my bucket, what a punk!
I chase him down, what a fuss,
Could have kept my lunch with no fuss!

With each wave, a memory's made,
In this dance of joy, I wade.
Laughter echoes, all around,
In the silence, stories abound!

Where Steps Fade Away

On the beach, my sandals go,
Leaving tracks where the breezes blow.
But one just vanished, like a trick,
Where's my shoe? That's quite the kick!

Sand gets sticky, like glue on toes,
I hop and dance, as everyone knows.
The tide's coming in, what a race,
Do I save my shoes, or just embrace?

Turtles watch in awe, I presume,
As I shuffle sideways, crushing the bloom.
Crabs are laughing, I can't deny,
This silly dance will catch the eye!

So here I stand, half in and half out,
What a sight, you can't have doubt.
When steps fade away, joy will sway,
And I'll be laughing, come what may!

In the Wake of Dreams

In the surf, I take a slip,
Down I go, what a fun trip!
Floating past shells on the tide,
I wave to the fish, they can't hide.

Sun-kissed moments, laughter's light,
I chase the gulls; oh, what a sight!
One snatches my sandwich with glee,
Screaming out, 'Hey, that's not for thee!'

The tides roll in, stealing my hat,
Who knew it would want a snack?
Joy sparkles like the sea with glee,
As I dance with the waves, wild and free!

Each splash feels like a gentle dream,
I glide over sand, a glistening beam.
In the wake of dreams, I find the fun,
Sandy stories shared, laughter not done!

Secrets Buried in the Shoreline

Sifting through grains, I find a toy,
An ancient relic, oh what joy!
But it's just a flip-flop, not a crown,
Covered in sand, it's wearing a frown.

Waves come crashing, secrets they hold,
Of summer days, both hot and cold.
I dig for treasures, shells, and bones,
But end up with sand and plenty of groans!

A seagull lands with a cheeky grin,
As I try searching for my win.
It squawks loudly, 'Hey, look at me!'
I throw a chip, and it laughs with glee!

Lost treasures may not be found today,
But humor lives in every play.
With secrets buried, I'll never tire,
In sandy moments, I find my fire!

Whispers of the Tide

As I slipped on the beach, oh what a sight,
My shoes flew away, in a wave of delight.
The tide laughed and danced, pulling me near,
I swore it was plotting my greatest career.

Sunbathers chuckled at my sandy parade,
I tried to look graceful but slipped and then swayed.
Seagulls watched closely, they seemed to conspire,
With shells in their beaks, I looked like a liar.

Waves whispered secrets of who's won the race,
While I lost my balance and wore mud on my face.
But oh, what a laugh, the ocean's own jest,
With each splash of water, I felt like a guest.

In the glow of the sun, I tried not to pout,
As my friends took pictures, their laughter a shout.
So I danced with the tide, going where it desired,
On this wobbly journey, I sure got inspired.

Marks of a Silent Walk

A quiet stroll turned to a slippery glide,
My flip-flops betrayed me, oh what a ride!
I stepped on a crab, he gave me a glare,
As I shouted, 'Hey buddy, this beach isn't fair!'

Sandcastles stood watch, with their towers so tall,
While I sank in the sand, made a laughable fall.
The tide giggled softly, like it knew all along,
That my silent walk was now more like a song.

My shadow skidded, like a cat on a tile,
While the beachball rolled by with a cheeky smile.
I leaped and I lunged, trying not to collide,
With a group of sunbathers on my comedic ride.

Oh, these silly footprints, they tell quite a tale,
Of misadventures in flip-flops, on a grand scale.
With laughter and joy, I'll treasure the spree,
Just a wanderer lost, but a happy one, me!

Tracks of the Wandering Soul

I ventured out boldly, my hat on askew,
While the sun beat down hard, as I danced with the dew.
Each step left a smudge, quite the curious art,
As I tried to impress, I just played the fool's part.

With a wave of my hand, I waved back at the tide,
But it swirled around me, refusing to hide.
A jellyfish floated, with a flouncy old jig,
I twirled past a kid, could've sworn he was big!

Every step that I took was a mix of delight,
As I slipped and I stumbled, what a clumsy sight!
I laughed with the seagulls, they seemed to agree,
That walking on sand is no walk by the sea.

So here I am now, in my sandy attire,
With grains in my hair, like I've set hearts on fire.
Though the journey was awkward, it brought me alive,
In the tracks of my wandering soul, I'll thrive!

Merely Moments Lost

A slip on the shoreline, a giggle resounds,
As I flew like a dolphin, just spinning around.
The surf was a magic carpet ride of a sort,
With laughter and waves, my own beach report.

I chased a bright crab, thought I was so keen,
But he turned and he dashed, didn't care for the scene.
The tide gave a chuckle, like it knew my show,
While I flailed through the foam, and my pride took a blow.

Seashells chimed in, my audience prime,
As they watched this grand act, all worthy of rhyme.
With each little tumble, a new memory made,
Writing my antics in sun, surf, and shade.

So here on the shore where I found such a thrill,
I'll cherish these moments, all the joy they instill.
With laughter my compass, I wander with glee,
In the chaos of fun, I find more of me!

www.ingramcontent.com/pod-product-compliance
Lightning Source LLC
Chambersburg PA
CBHW072216070526
44585CB00015B/1370